TRUE
Presence

SELINA WARD

BALBOA.
PRESS
A DIVISION OF HAY HOUSE

Balboa Press books may be ordered through booksellers or by contacting:

Balboa Press
A Division of Hay House
1663 Liberty Drive
Bloomington, IN 47403
www.balboapress.com.au
1 (877) 407-4847

Print information available on the last page.

ISBN: 978-1-5043-1320-9 (sc)
ISBN: 978-1-5043-1321-6 (e)

Balboa Press rev. date: 06/08/2018

Contents

Introduction

This book of poems is dedicated to Gail and Caleb Jones who left this world within four months of each other, forever together.

They taught me many things, but two stand out above the rest. The first was to be true to myself and the second was to find my own piece of paradise. Gail believed in fore filling your dreams, and most of all being true to yourself while doing it. And Caleb, though only young was as his mother was, true to himself.

He didn't express himself in the manner that others expected him to. At a family gathering I had offered him a hug and he said no. But later on, he showed his affection by grabbing my hand and gently pressing it to his cheek while closing his eye's and smiling. I looked at Gail in confusion and she informed me that that was Caleb's version of a hug. In that moment I felt my heart hurt with love for him. At such a young age he got it. You don't have to act, feel or be the same as anyone else. As long as you were true to yourself and honest about it then all would be good.

Many adults struggle to achieve this but at the age of 1 1/2 he truly understood it and lived by it. Gail and Caleb taught me that you don't have to conform to society and what others expected and wanted from you. That you could also do what is right for yourself at that moment in time. As long as it didn't hurt or endanger others it would all be ok.

I never thought when we lost you both that I would ever be content, happy or at peace again. It was like my inner world had ceased to exist, knowing I'd never hug either of you again, hear your laughter or do silly things like sumo wrestling. Even though I still sometimes cry, I find something to smile or laugh at every day. I live my life for me and the pleasure a day and nature gives' me. I treat others how I want to be treated. But what has got me through is something Gail said to me. That I can't live my life for others, I had to live it for myself. To be true to myself and if I was undecided about something, then in the end it had to be right for me first and last or I would never be happy. I've done my best to live by this moto and I felt the need to share my inner thoughts and journey to achieve what I feel was Gail's legacy, because she was right. I miss you both every day and this is my way of thanking you for how you guided and encouraged with total honesty. Never wavering from your beliefs, true to your heart and soul. Forever young you both shall be, eternally etched in time.

Etched in Time

The glorious sunset

Setting fire to the sky

The soft velvet feel of

A blood red rose petal

The chatter of nature on the wind

The musical sound of

Children's laughter

The mystical appearance of the universe

On a clear starry night

The extravagance of your beauty

Is etched in time

Our Angel

I held your hand
As you lay there still as night
Your angelic body
White against white

Taking your last stand
As a single tear
Rolled down your cheek

I knew then
This was good-bye
Accepting it was time
For you to go

I found hard
Thinking why
Why you

And then realising
I wouldn't wish this on anyone else
Not even my worst enemy

As time has passed
You have never been far
From my mind
The memory of you
Is powerful
Invoking smiles and laughter
With every though of you

The occasional tear still
Wells in my eyes
Forever in my heart
you will remain

An angel sent
To bless our lives

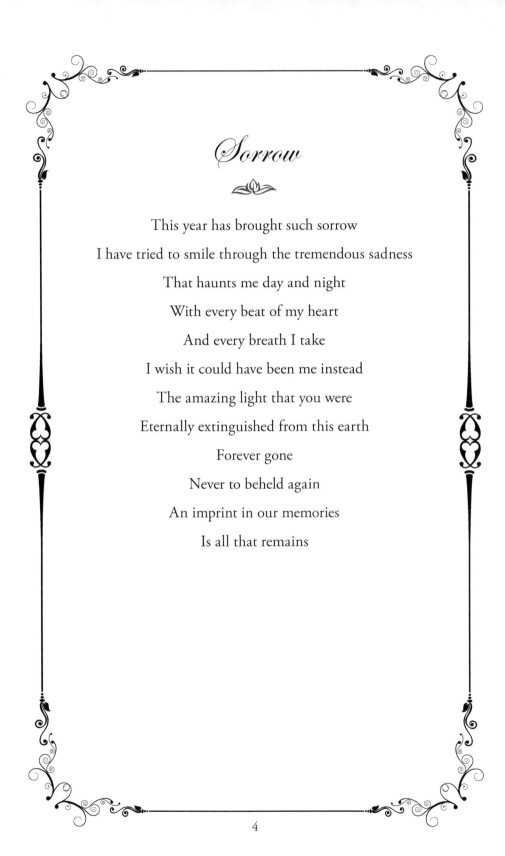

Sorrow

This year has brought such sorrow

I have tried to smile through the tremendous sadness

That haunts me day and night

With every beat of my heart

And every breath I take

I wish it could have been me instead

The amazing light that you were

Eternally extinguished from this earth

Forever gone

Never to beheld again

An imprint in our memories

Is all that remains

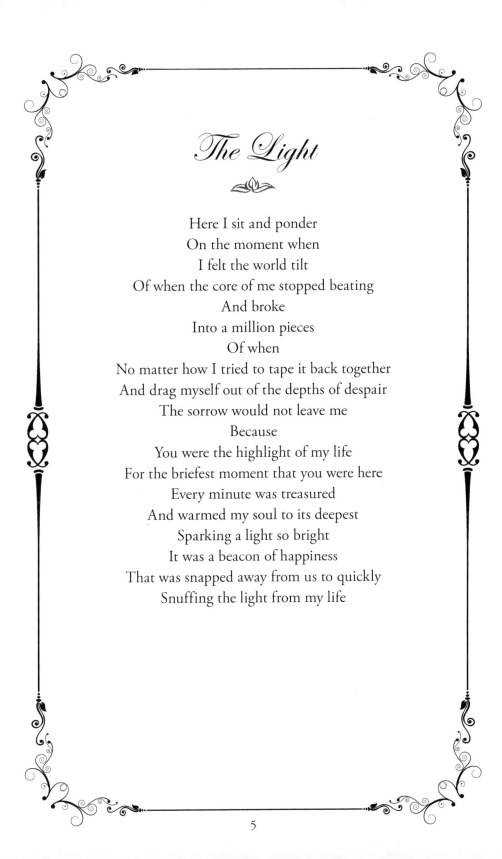

The Light

Here I sit and ponder
On the moment when
I felt the world tilt
Of when the core of me stopped beating
And broke
Into a million pieces
Of when
No matter how I tried to tape it back together
And drag myself out of the depths of despair
The sorrow would not leave me
Because
You were the highlight of my life
For the briefest moment that you were here
Every minute was treasured
And warmed my soul to its deepest
Sparking a light so bright
It was a beacon of happiness
That was snapped away from us to quickly
Snuffing the light from my life

Emptiness

Loneliness is such an empty feeling

It has nothing to do with your head

And everything to do with your heart and soul

It's that pain

You know

The one that feels like someone is trying

To squeeze the life out of you

It's the feeling that makes you sad

So sad

That you eventually lose the smile from your eyes

You wonder how long will this last

A few months

A year

Maybe ten

I want the emptiness to end

But I don't know how to end it

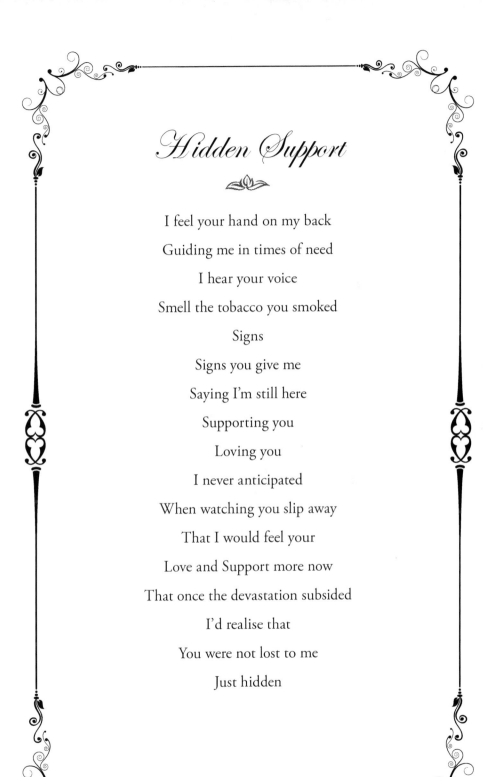

Hidden Support

I feel your hand on my back

Guiding me in times of need

I hear your voice

Smell the tobacco you smoked

Signs

Signs you give me

Saying I'm still here

Supporting you

Loving you

I never anticipated

When watching you slip away

That I would feel your

Love and Support more now

That once the devastation subsided

I'd realise that

You were not lost to me

Just hidden

Times Irrelevant

It's amazing how time becomes irrelevant
How one little piece of news
Makes your world stand still
To think
Do I run?
Do I stand and fight?
Or do I ride the waves
And see where I end up
You realize that you're not going to run
That it's only fair to stand your ground
And ride the waves
To trust blindly that when you fall
Someone will be there
Suddenly you know
That there will always be someone
No matter how alone you feel
You truly never are
And that you really should say
"I love you"
To the people you love
You never know what tomorrow will bring

You're My Light

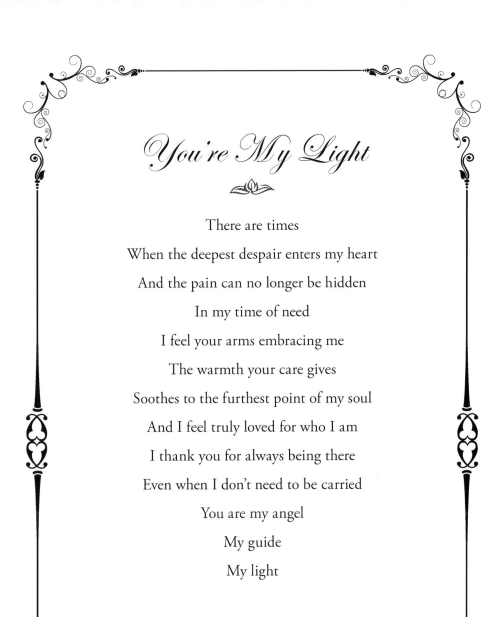

There are times

When the deepest despair enters my heart

And the pain can no longer be hidden

In my time of need

I feel your arms embracing me

The warmth your care gives

Soothes to the furthest point of my soul

And I feel truly loved for who I am

I thank you for always being there

Even when I don't need to be carried

You are my angel

My guide

My light

Such Peace

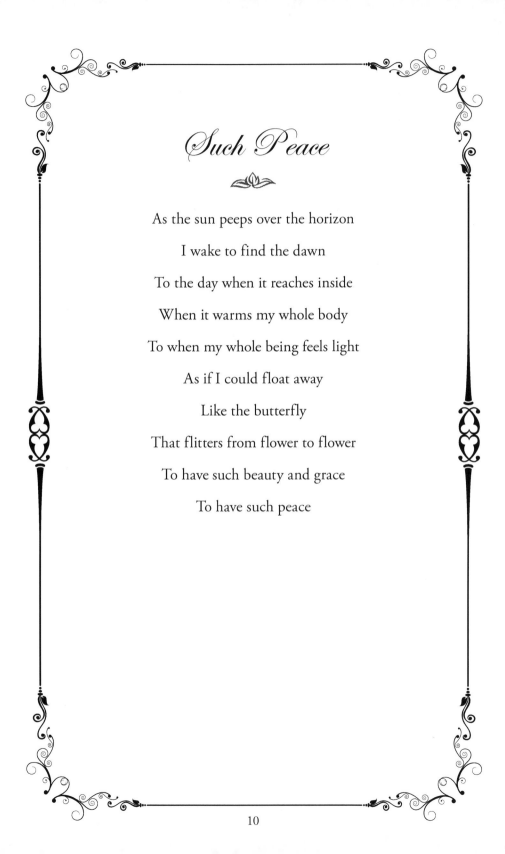

As the sun peeps over the horizon

I wake to find the dawn

To the day when it reaches inside

When it warms my whole body

To when my whole being feels light

As if I could float away

Like the butterfly

That flitters from flower to flower

To have such beauty and grace

To have such peace

Find your Peace

You need to find your place of peace

Your piece of paradise

A place you can heal and nurture yourself

You will know it when you find it

It warms you from within

A smile gracing your face without thought

To feel your pain and to accept it

To learn from it

And move forward

Growing into the beautiful soul

You have always been

Hidden deep within

A Time for Reflection

There will always be times in your life
When you sit and reflect

There is always a need to stop
To smell nature at its best
To see how far you have come

To feel growth
To hear your truth from within
To taste your achievements
No matter how small

Stop and reflect
Look at what is happening around you
Something as simple as
The sun hitting a drop of water
Bringing it to life
Like a sparkling jewel

Sometimes
There is a need to take joy in the little things
It helps
When all else seems untouchable
It gives perspective
It nurtures the soul
Giving peace and acceptance

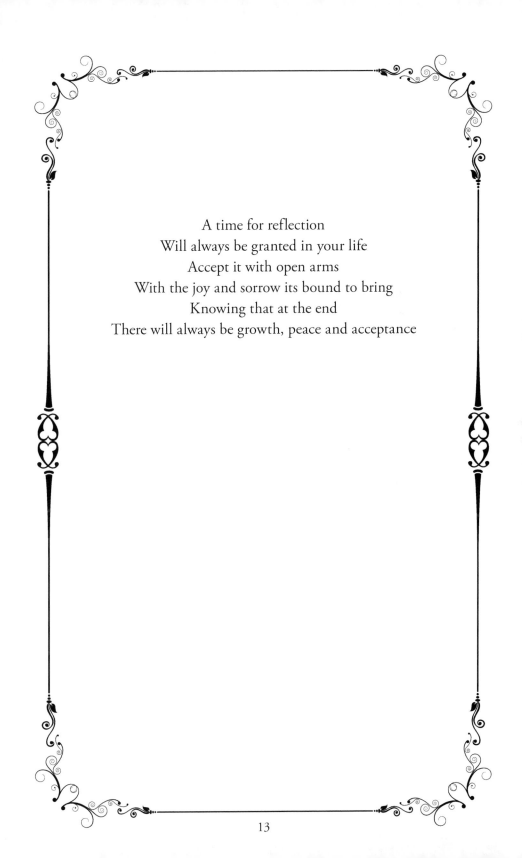

A time for reflection
Will always be granted in your life
Accept it with open arms
With the joy and sorrow its bound to bring
Knowing that at the end
There will always be growth, peace and acceptance

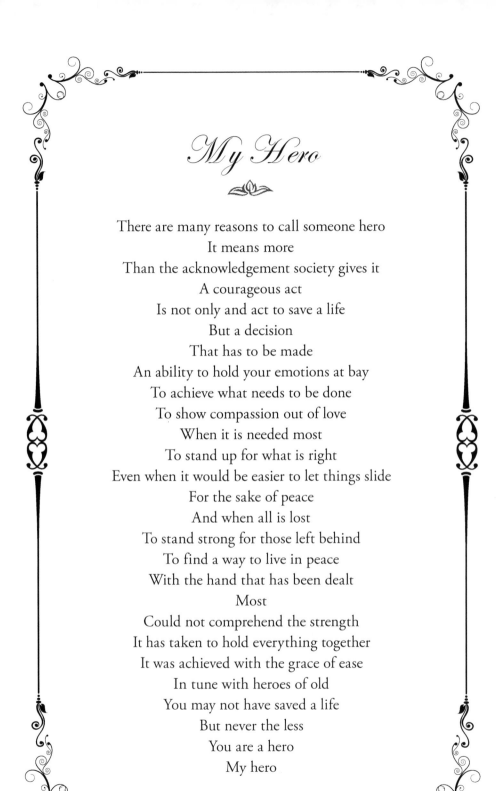

My Hero

There are many reasons to call someone hero
It means more
Than the acknowledgement society gives it
A courageous act
Is not only and act to save a life
But a decision
That has to be made
An ability to hold your emotions at bay
To achieve what needs to be done
To show compassion out of love
When it is needed most
To stand up for what is right
Even when it would be easier to let things slide
For the sake of peace
And when all is lost
To stand strong for those left behind
To find a way to live in peace
With the hand that has been dealt
Most
Could not comprehend the strength
It has taken to hold everything together
It was achieved with the grace of ease
In tune with heroes of old
You may not have saved a life
But never the less
You are a hero
My hero

Supporting Me

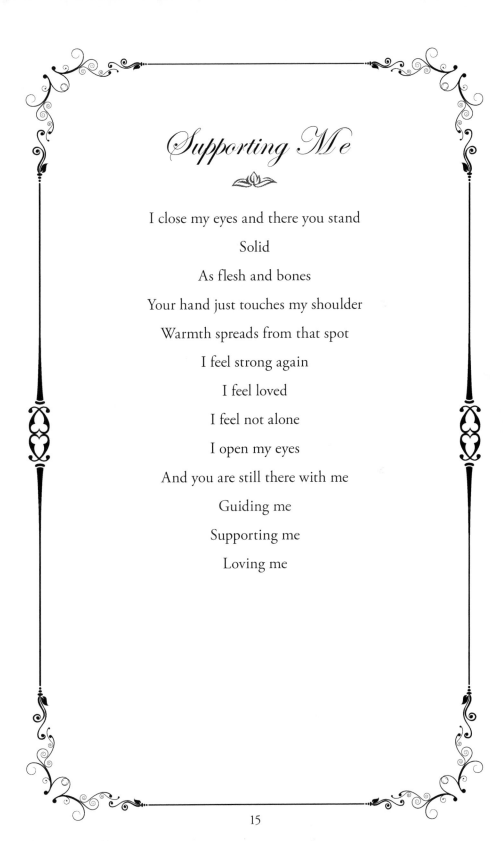

I close my eyes and there you stand

Solid

As flesh and bones

Your hand just touches my shoulder

Warmth spreads from that spot

I feel strong again

I feel loved

I feel not alone

I open my eyes

And you are still there with me

Guiding me

Supporting me

Loving me

Cherished Memories

I have many memories of your life

And I draw on those when I think of you

The devastation and pain of losing you

I didn't think would ever leave me

As time passes

The more I think of the times we've shared

I smile

Realizing my grief has turned to sadness

I smile

At all the cherished memories

I have of you to look back on

I smile

With sadness and love

But I smile

Day Dream

As the stream trickles passed

In the soft lush green grass

Along its banks

I stand

Watching butterflies

Dance among the wild flowers

Across the way

Taking me into a day dream

Serenity

Enters my soul

As the cool breeze whips around me

I close my eyes

And lose myself in the dream

Smiling towards the heavens

Your whisper

Touches my skin

Be happy my love

Our Time Here is so Short

I sit and watch children play

They just immerse themselves in life

With no fear

No hesitation

Embracing with lustre

Showing how they feel

With no restraint

Allowing their imagination to run free

No limitations

As adults we should take more notice

Our time here is so short

And as a butterfly Flies by

I take the time to watch it

Realizing that it's time to start living

To embrace and immerse myself

In life's experiences

This Feeling Inside

This feeling inside is painful
A knot of apprehension unfolding
Into a fear of what is around the corner
Willing yourself to take the next step
To just put one foot in front of the other
Listening to the voice inside saying it's time
Don't be afraid
All your wishes, dreams and hopes
Are about to come true
Be brave
Have faith
Don't retreat to your safe haven
Embrace this feeling
The intensity of it
Even though it is frightening
It is also empowering
It helps you grow to be a better person
Ok
Now hold your breath
It's time to take that
Step into the unknown

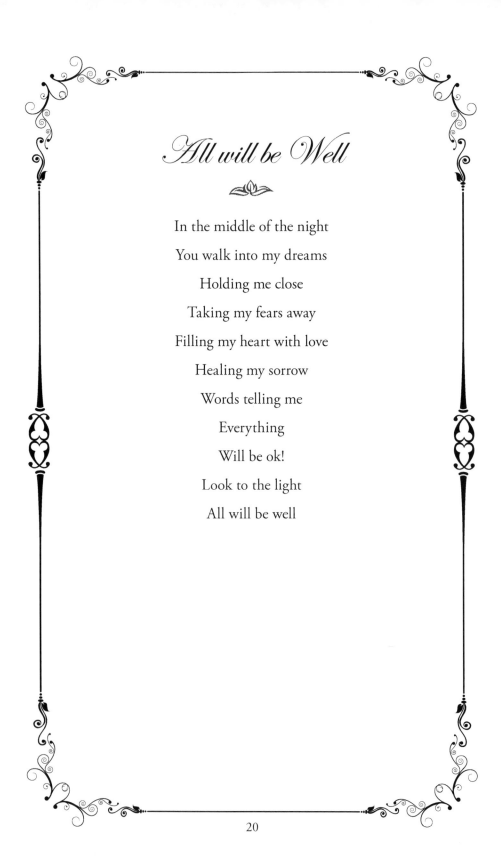

All will be Well

In the middle of the night

You walk into my dreams

Holding me close

Taking my fears away

Filling my heart with love

Healing my sorrow

Words telling me

Everything

Will be ok!

Look to the light

All will be well

Faith

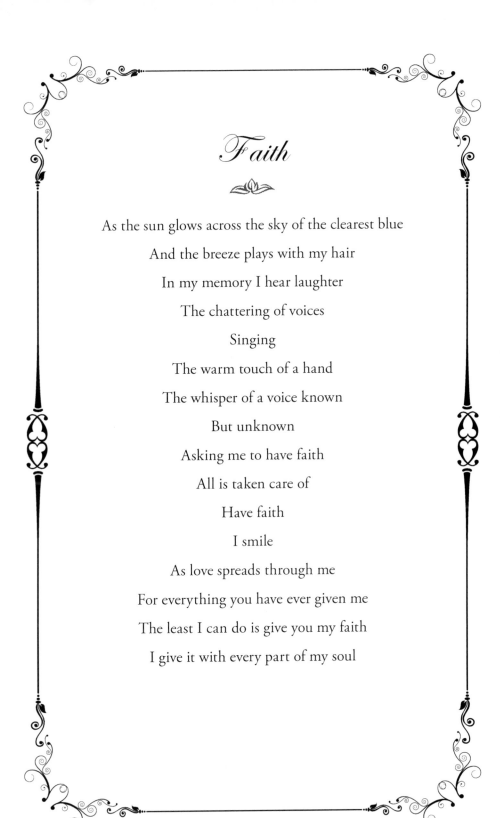

As the sun glows across the sky of the clearest blue

And the breeze plays with my hair

In my memory I hear laughter

The chattering of voices

Singing

The warm touch of a hand

The whisper of a voice known

But unknown

Asking me to have faith

All is taken care of

Have faith

I smile

As love spreads through me

For everything you have ever given me

The least I can do is give you my faith

I give it with every part of my soul

To Cleanse the Soul

When tragedy entered my life
And things seem to be too much
A pressure building
And building
Waiting to explode from within
Nature was my escape
I'd go to the mountains and surround myself with it
A walk in the park or along the bush track
I'd find a place to stand or sit and gaze out at the sight before me
I'd breath in the air so deeply it was audible
Closing my eyes and raising my face to the sky
In and out
Slowly
Smelling and even tasting
The mix of eucalyptus and pine trees
Hearing the rustle of the leaves as the wind weaves through them
Touching the soft petal of the many flowers along the way
Or feeling the roughness of the bark under my fingers
The heat of the rock I'd chosen to sit on
Watching the lizards, birds and on the odd occasion
If you were quiet enough
echidnas foraging in the undergrowth
It would ease the pain deep within
I could feel all my worries
My sadness
My loneliness
Slowly seeping away from my soul
Though not fully at peace

But enough
Enough to go on and face the world
Enough to put on the brave happy face needed
Because If this was how I felt
Then I could only imagine how he felt
And as a sister all I could give him
Was my support
I gave it gladly and unconditionally
And I would do it all over again
Just as nature is there for me
I'll be there for him

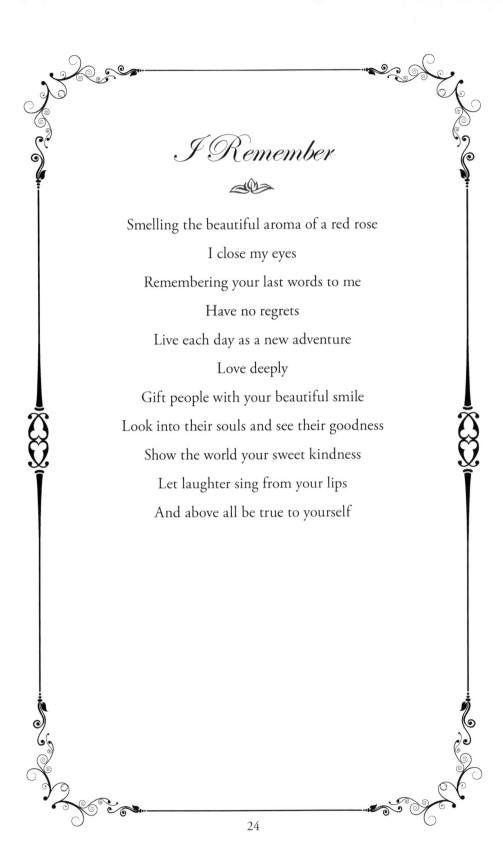

I Remember

Smelling the beautiful aroma of a red rose

I close my eyes

Remembering your last words to me

Have no regrets

Live each day as a new adventure

Love deeply

Gift people with your beautiful smile

Look into their souls and see their goodness

Show the world your sweet kindness

Let laughter sing from your lips

And above all be true to yourself

Keep Climbing

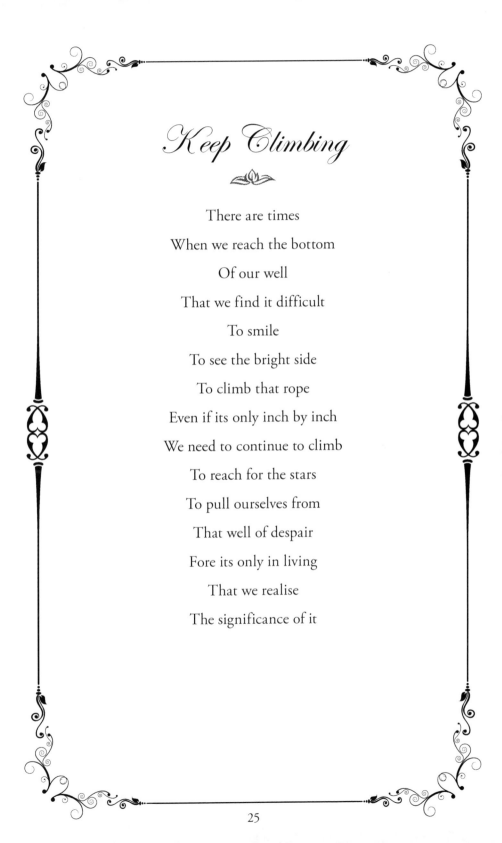

There are times

When we reach the bottom

Of our well

That we find it difficult

To smile

To see the bright side

To climb that rope

Even if its only inch by inch

We need to continue to climb

To reach for the stars

To pull ourselves from

That well of despair

Fore its only in living

That we realise

The significance of it

My Journey Begins

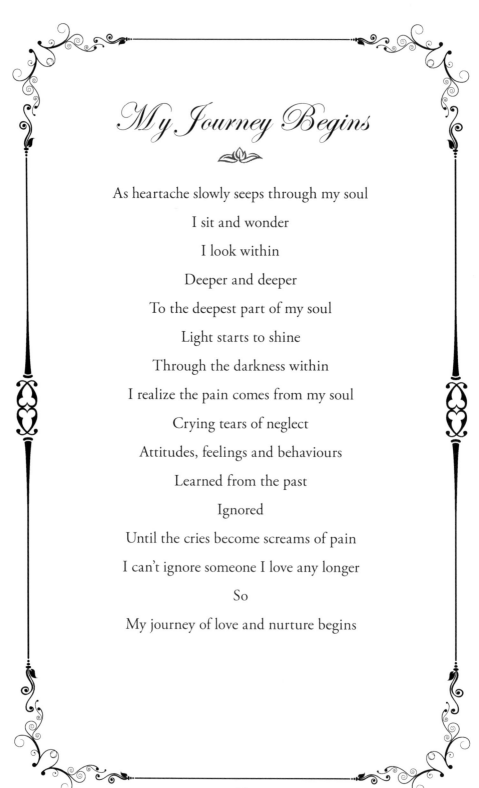

As heartache slowly seeps through my soul

I sit and wonder

I look within

Deeper and deeper

To the deepest part of my soul

Light starts to shine

Through the darkness within

I realize the pain comes from my soul

Crying tears of neglect

Attitudes, feelings and behaviours

Learned from the past

Ignored

Until the cries become screams of pain

I can't ignore someone I love any longer

So

My journey of love and nurture begins

Change

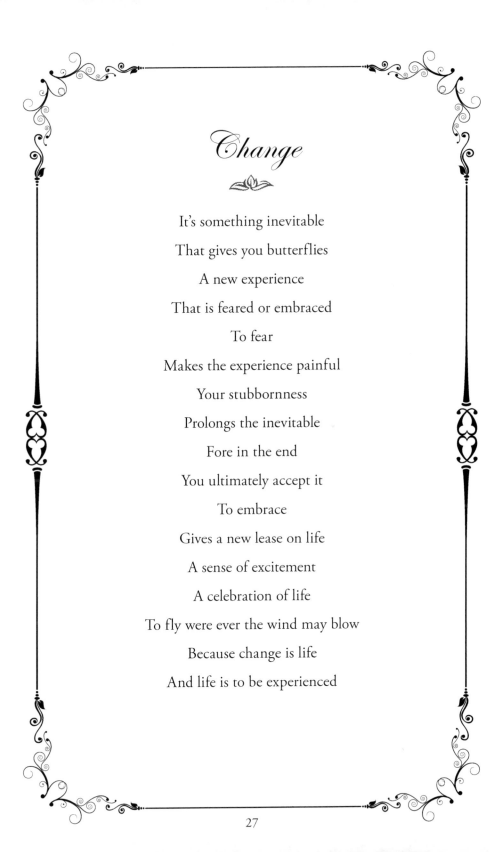

It's something inevitable

That gives you butterflies

A new experience

That is feared or embraced

To fear

Makes the experience painful

Your stubbornness

Prolongs the inevitable

Fore in the end

You ultimately accept it

To embrace

Gives a new lease on life

A sense of excitement

A celebration of life

To fly were ever the wind may blow

Because change is life

And life is to be experienced

Conquering All

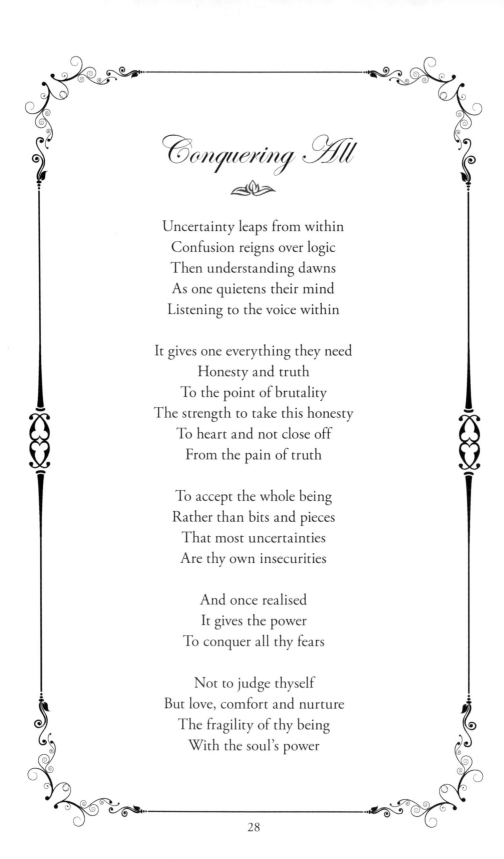

Uncertainty leaps from within
Confusion reigns over logic
Then understanding dawns
As one quietens their mind
Listening to the voice within

It gives one everything they need
Honesty and truth
To the point of brutality
The strength to take this honesty
To heart and not close off
From the pain of truth

To accept the whole being
Rather than bits and pieces
That most uncertainties
Are thy own insecurities

And once realised
It gives the power
To conquer all thy fears

Not to judge thyself
But love, comfort and nurture
The fragility of thy being
With the soul's power

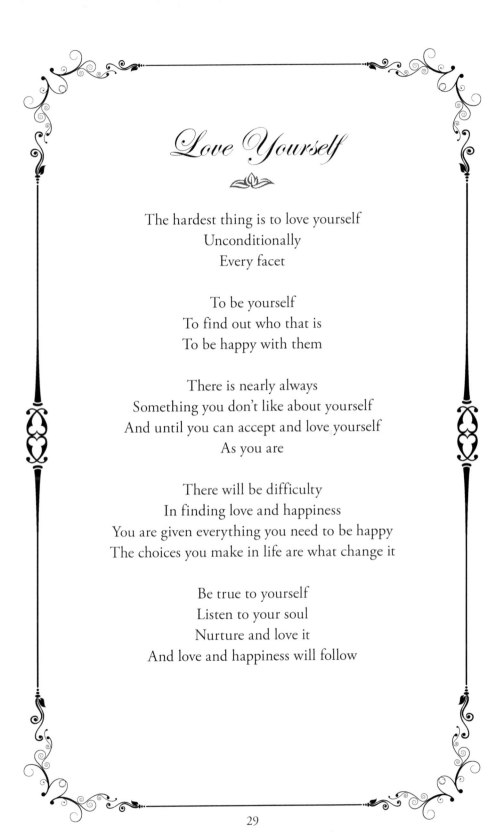

Love Yourself

The hardest thing is to love yourself
Unconditionally
Every facet

To be yourself
To find out who that is
To be happy with them

There is nearly always
Something you don't like about yourself
And until you can accept and love yourself
As you are

There will be difficulty
In finding love and happiness
You are given everything you need to be happy
The choices you make in life are what change it

Be true to yourself
Listen to your soul
Nurture and love it
And love and happiness will follow

Journey of Light

Some days are harder than others
We get caught up in the race of expectations
That we have for ourselves
That our family wants for us
That society expects from us

It seems an endless stream of pressure
Everything closing in forming a wall of impressions
A river of feelings rushing around any obstacle
The sense to slow down
The need to look

And as I retreat to a place of inner peace
I look over my mind
Gathering my thoughts
Letting each go until it flows like a river

Being washed by pure energy
Swirling around your whole body
Inside and out
Going where ever the flow takes you
Immersing yourself in the journey
A journey of discovery
A journey of knowledge
A journey of light

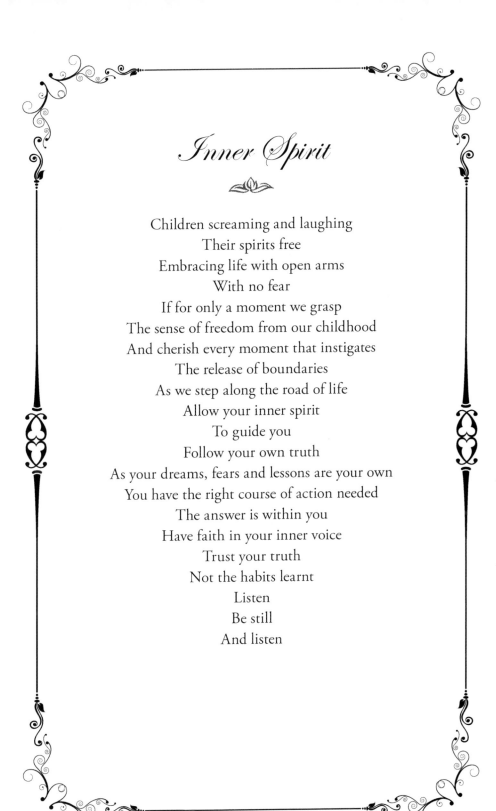

Inner Spirit

Children screaming and laughing
Their spirits free
Embracing life with open arms
With no fear
If for only a moment we grasp
The sense of freedom from our childhood
And cherish every moment that instigates
The release of boundaries
As we step along the road of life
Allow your inner spirit
To guide you
Follow your own truth
As your dreams, fears and lessons are your own
You have the right course of action needed
The answer is within you
Have faith in your inner voice
Trust your truth
Not the habits learnt
Listen
Be still
And listen

The Key

My life is free

With every step I take

With every thought I have

With every smell, taste and sight

I choose to concentrate on the light

And not the darkness that enters everyday life

To smile in the face of adversity

And to send love

In any situation I've found myself in

Even the most painful

There has always been light

I look for the good

And I find myself surrounded by beauty

As I smell the roses

I smile as the memories pass before my eyes

I have no regrets and a blessed life

The key is love

Time

Time is the one thing that governs all things
In all forms of life
It takes time to grow a plant
From seed, to seedling, to plant
In all its glory
And each plant takes its own sweet time
To reach all that glory
The beauty of each stage missed
Due to life as we call it
Too busy, negative thoughts and actions
Never enough time it seems
As we get tied up with misunderstanding the meaning
Only looking from one perspective
Yes
Everything takes time
But
Each moment is glorious in its own right
And
Each moment leads into the next
A step
An action
A thought
All took time
But
Led us to where we are today
To who we are
You may not yet be where you want to be

But
Time will certainly take you there
Really
It's up to you
How you fill those moments
that take you there
Choose positive over negative
Make use of the time available to you
It's time to stop being angry with it
And revel in it instead
Enjoy every moment
For the wonder it is

New Beginnings

As the sun rises and the flowers open

Their petals embracing the rays of light

A new year begins allowing a fresh start

We open ourselves up for new beginnings

We say good-bye to the past

And leave it where it belongs

The heart is a fragile thing

But our soul is strong

Everything will heal over time

If you only allow love in

We have belief, faith and love within ourselves

The most powerful being love

Fore it can conquer all

True Presence

The greatest gift you can offer loved one's
Is your true presence
From the first time I met you
It never wavered
You taught me to be comfortable in my own skin
That it was ok to be me
I truly believe in my heart
That your presence was a gift to the world
And those you touched will not forget
How you enriched their lives
There will be moments when we miss you so much
That we just want to pluck you from our memory
And hug you for real one more time
And at times we will smile
In loving memory of who you were
Straight down the line
No beating around the bush
True to your presence

Your Little Piece of Paradise

There's this house in north Brisbane where we stay

It looks like any other street in the suburbs

Until you step into the dining room

And look out the expanse of glass

There is a wooden deck overlooking nature

A variety of birds visit everyday

Along with the lizards

That like to take a dip in the pool

I never thought

I would find peace and tranquillity in the city

But here

You would think you were in the countryside

Your little piece of paradise

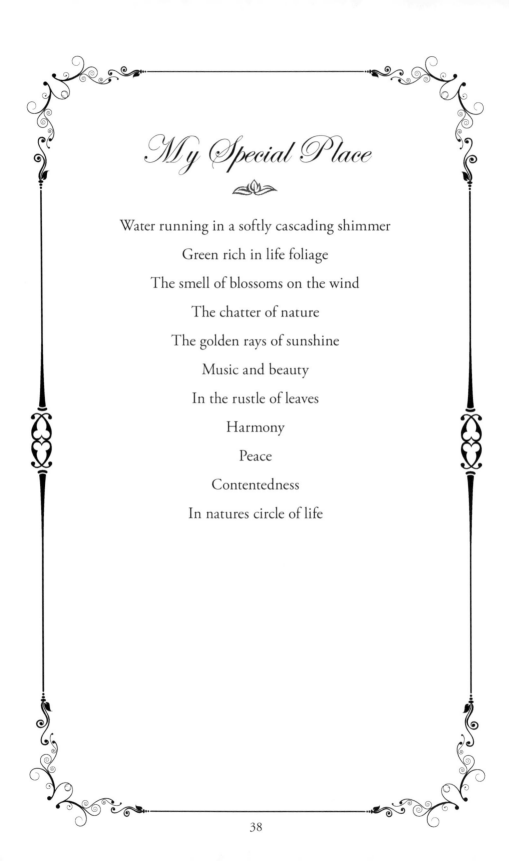

My Special Place

Water running in a softly cascading shimmer

Green rich in life foliage

The smell of blossoms on the wind

The chatter of nature

The golden rays of sunshine

Music and beauty

In the rustle of leaves

Harmony

Peace

Contentedness

In natures circle of life

Family

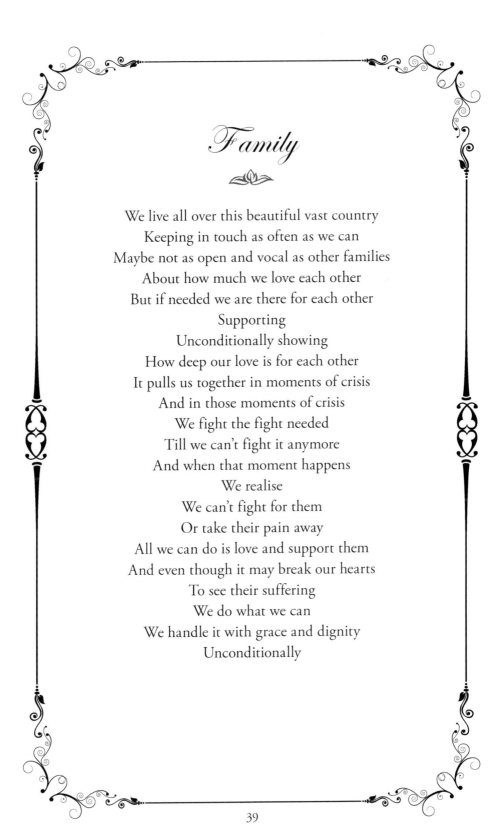

We live all over this beautiful vast country
Keeping in touch as often as we can
Maybe not as open and vocal as other families
About how much we love each other
But if needed we are there for each other
Supporting
Unconditionally showing
How deep our love is for each other
It pulls us together in moments of crisis
And in those moments of crisis
We fight the fight needed
Till we can't fight it anymore
And when that moment happens
We realise
We can't fight for them
Or take their pain away
All we can do is love and support them
And even though it may break our hearts
To see their suffering
We do what we can
We handle it with grace and dignity
Unconditionally

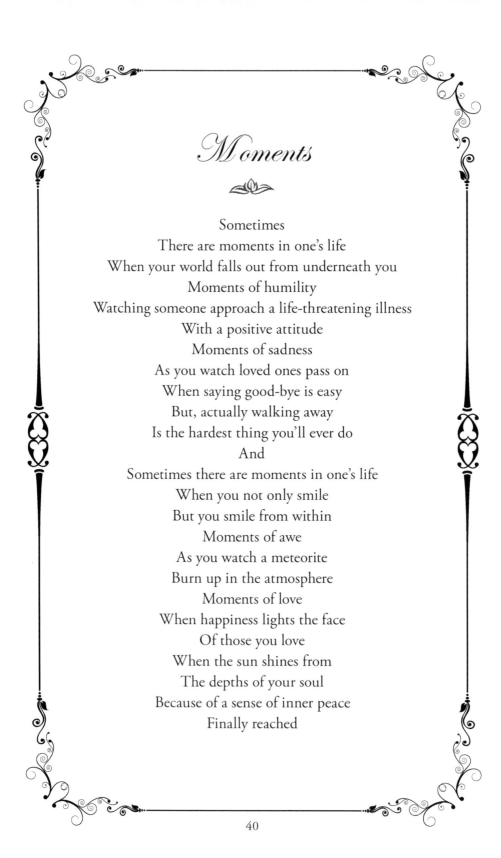

Moments

Sometimes
There are moments in one's life
When your world falls out from underneath you
Moments of humility
Watching someone approach a life-threatening illness
With a positive attitude
Moments of sadness
As you watch loved ones pass on
When saying good-bye is easy
But, actually walking away
Is the hardest thing you'll ever do
And
Sometimes there are moments in one's life
When you not only smile
But you smile from within
Moments of awe
As you watch a meteorite
Burn up in the atmosphere
Moments of love
When happiness lights the face
Of those you love
When the sun shines from
The depths of your soul
Because of a sense of inner peace
Finally reached

Not Perfect

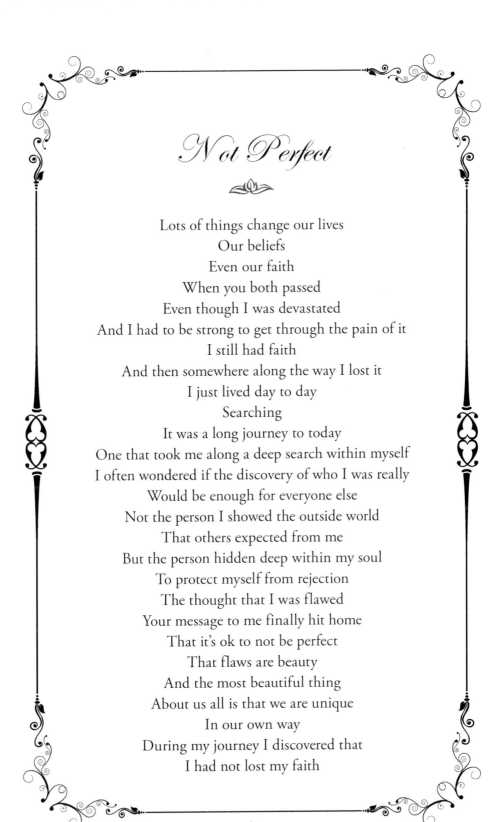

Lots of things change our lives
Our beliefs
Even our faith
When you both passed
Even though I was devastated
And I had to be strong to get through the pain of it
I still had faith
And then somewhere along the way I lost it
I just lived day to day
Searching
It was a long journey to today
One that took me along a deep search within myself
I often wondered if the discovery of who I was really
Would be enough for everyone else
Not the person I showed the outside world
That others expected from me
But the person hidden deep within my soul
To protect myself from rejection
The thought that I was flawed
Your message to me finally hit home
That it's ok to not be perfect
That flaws are beauty
And the most beautiful thing
About us all is that we are unique
In our own way
During my journey I discovered that
I had not lost my faith

It had just change
And that I'm just like everyone else
Not perfect or flawed
But unique

Printed in the United States
By Bookmasters